MAY 2010

W9-BNS-165

Pebble® Bilingüe/Bilingual Plus

Tiburones/Sharks

Gran tiburón blanco / Great White Shark

por/by Deborah Nuzzolo

Editor Consultor/Consulting Editor: Dra. Gail Saunders-Smith

Consultor/Consultant: Jody Rake, member
Southwest Marine/Aquatic Educators' Association

CAPSTONE PRESS
a capstone imprint

Pebble Plus is published by Capstone Press,
151 Good Counsel Drive, P.O. Box 669, Mankato, Minnesota 56002.
www.capstonepress.com

092009
005618CGS10

 Books published by Capstone Press are manufactured with
paper containing at least 10 percent post-consumer waste.

Library of Congress Cataloging-in-Publication Data
Nuzzolo, Deborah.
  [Great white shark. Spanish & English]
  Gran tiburón blanco = Great white shark / por/by Deborah Nuzzolo.
  p. cm. — (Pebble plus bilingüe/bilingual. Tiburones/sharks)
  Includes index.
  Summary: "Simple text and photographs present great white sharks, their body parts, and their
behavior — in both English and Spanish" — Provided by publisher.
  ISBN 978-1-4296-4801-1 (library binding)
  1. White shark — Juvenile literature. I. Title. II. Title: Great white shark. III. Series.
QL638.95.L3N8818 2010
597.3'3 — dc22   2009037867

Editorial Credits
Megan Peterson, editor; Strictly Spanish, translation services; Katy Kudela, bilingual editor;
    Ted Williams, set designer; Kyle Grenz, book designer; Jo Miller, photo researcher;
    Eric Manske and Danielle Ceminsky, production specialists

Photo Credits
Bruce Coleman Inc./Maris Kazmers, 19; Ron & Valerie Taylor, 10–11
Getty Images Inc./Minden Pictures/Mike Perry, 7; Photographer's Choice/David Nardini, cover;
    Science Faction/Stephen Frink, 17
Nature Picture Library/Doc White, 14–15
Shutterstock/Simone Conti, backgrounds
SuperStock, Inc./Pacific Stock, 4–5
Tom Stack & Associates, Inc./Dave Fleetham, 9, 13
Visuals Unlimited/Brandon Cole, 20–21; Marty Snyderman, 1

Note to Parents and Teachers

The Tiburones/Sharks set supports national science standards related to the
characteristics and behavior of animals. This book describes and illustrates great white
sharks in both English and Spanish. The images support early readers in understanding
the text. The repetition of words and phrases helps early readers learn new words. This
book also introduces early readers to subject-specific vocabulary words, which are
defined in the Glossary section. Early readers may need assistance to read some words
and to use the Table of Contents, Glossary, Internet Sites, and Index sections of the book.

Table of Contents

Tabla de contenidos

Fearsome Fish

Great white sharks are fearsome fish. They are the largest hunting fish in the world.

Peces temibles

Los grandes tiburones blancos son peces temibles. Son los peces cazadores más grandes del mundo.

Great whites live worldwide

in mostly cool water.

They swim along the shore

to search for food.

Los tiburones blancos viven en todas

partes del mundo, mayormente en aguas

frías. Ellos nadan a lo largo de la orilla

en búsqueda de comida.

Great White Shark Pups

Great white shark pups are born
live. Between two and 10 pups
are born at one time.

Crías del gran tiburón blanco

Las crías del gran tiburón blanco
nacen vivas. Entre dos y 10 crías
nacen al mismo tiempo.

Shark pups live and grow
on their own. Great white
sharks live about 25 years.

Las crías de tiburón viven y crecen
por su cuenta. Los tiburones blancos
viven alrededor de 25 años.

What They Look Like

Great white sharks have white undersides and gray backs. The gray color blends in with the ocean floor.

A qué se parecen

La parte inferior de los tiburones blancos es blanca y la parte superior es gris. El color gris armoniza con el suelo del océano.

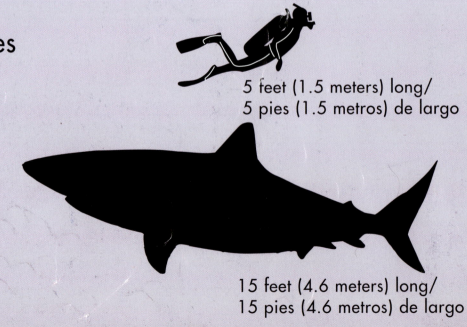

5 feet (1.5 meters) long/
5 pies (1.5 metros) de largo

15 feet (4.6 meters) long/
15 pies (4.6 metros) de largo

Great white shark bodies look like footballs. This smooth shape helps great whites speed after prey.

Los cuerpos de los grandes tiburones blancos se parecen a un balón de fútbol americano. Esta forma suave ayuda a los tiburones blancos a nadar con velocidad detrás de su presa.

Great white sharks have a
nostril on each side of their
snout. They use their sense
of smell to find prey.

Los tiburones blancos tienen una
fosa nasal a cada lado de su
hocico. Usan el sentido del
olfato para encontrar presas.

**nostril/
fosa nasal**

17

Hunting

Great white sharks hunt

seals, sea lions, and dolphins.

They can jump out of the water

to catch prey.

Caza

Los grandes tiburones blancos cazan

focas, lobos marinos y delfines.

Ellos pueden saltar fuera del agua

para atrapar a su presa.

Great white sharks bite prey
with many sharp teeth.
Few animals can escape
the jaws of this ocean hunter.

Los tiburones blancos muerden a su presa
con muchos dientes filosos. Muy pocos
animales pueden escapar las mandíbulas
de este cazador del océano.

Glossary

escape — to get away from

fearsome — frightening or scary

hunt — to chase and kill animals for food

nostril — an opening in a shark's nose through which it smells

prey — an animal hunted by another animal for food

pup — a young shark

shore — the place where the water meets land; many sharks swim in the shallow water near the shore.

smooth — even and free from bumps

snout — the long front part of a shark's head that includes the nose, mouth, and jaws

Internet Sites

FactHound offers a safe, fun way to find Internet sites related to this book. All of the sites on FactHound have been researched by our staff.

Here's all you do:

Visit *www.facthound.com*

FactHound will fetch the best sites for you!

Glosario

cazar — perseguir y matar animales para comer

la cría — un tiburón joven

escapar — huir de algo o alguien

la fosa nasal — un orificio en la nariz de un tiburón por el cual huele

el hocico — la parte larga frontal de la cabeza de un tiburón que incluye la nariz, la boca y las mandíbulas

la orilla — el lugar donde el agua se junta con la tierra; muchos tiburones nadan en el agua poco profunda cerca de la orilla.

la presa — un animal cazado por otro para comérselo

suave — parejo y libre de bultos

temible — que produce temor o miedo

Sitios de Internet

FactHound brinda una forma segura y divertida de encontrar sitios de Internet relacionados con este libro. Todos los sitios en FactHound han sido investigados por nuestro personal.

Esto es todo lo que tú necesitas hacer:

Visita *www.facthound.com*

¡FactHound buscará los mejores sitios para ti!

Index

Índice